A Crabtree Branches Book

CATCH the Wave

BIG WAVE SURFING

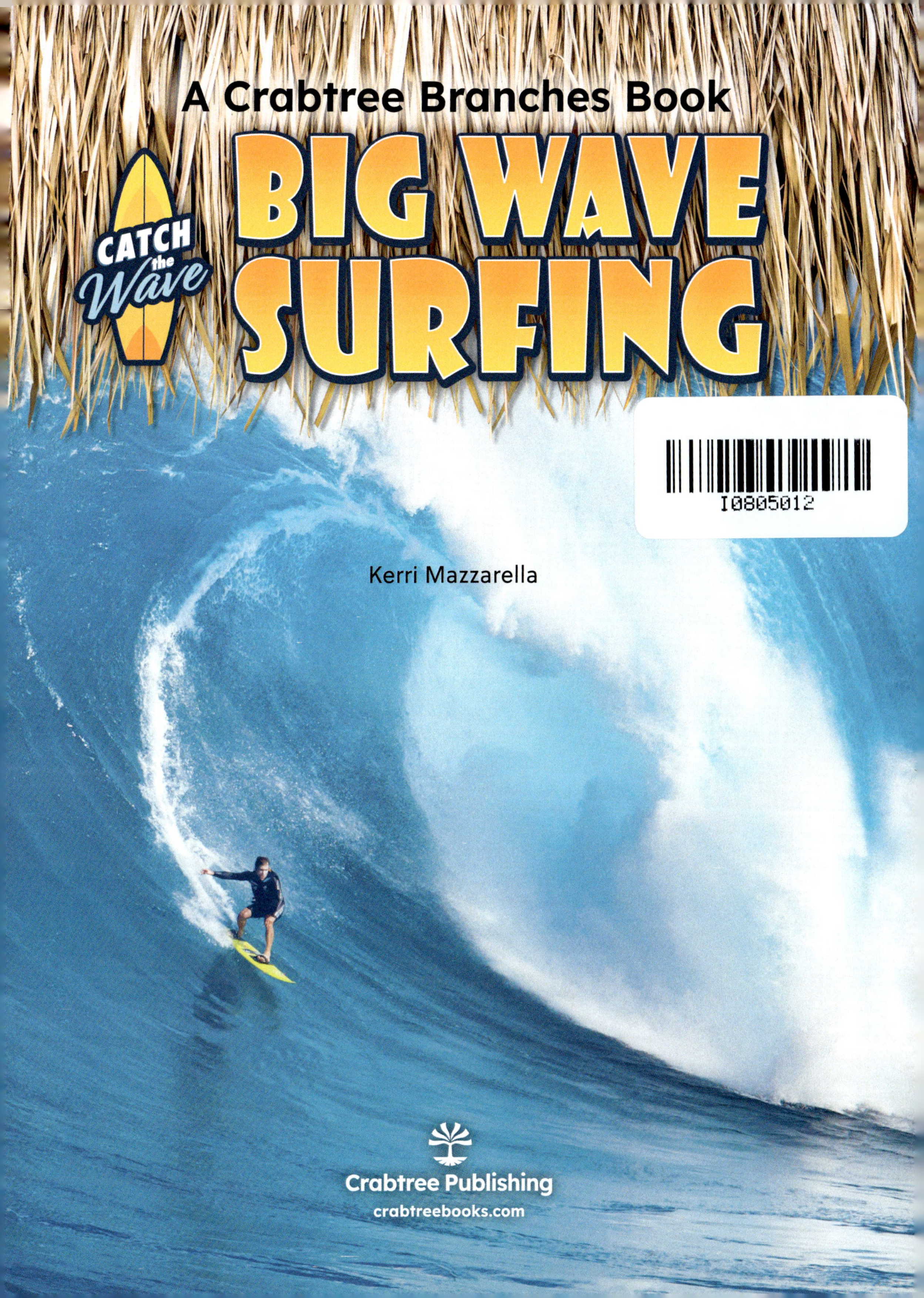

Kerri Mazzarella

Crabtree Publishing
crabtreebooks.com

School-to-Home Support for Caregivers and Teachers

This high-interest book is designed to motivate striving students with engaging topics while building fluency, vocabulary, and an interest in reading. Here are a few questions and activities to help the reader build upon his or her comprehension skills.

Before Reading:

- *What do I think this book is about?*
- *What do I know about this topic?*
- *What do I want to learn about this topic?*
- *Why am I reading this book?*

During Reading:

- *I wonder why...*
- *I'm curious to know...*
- *How is this like something I already know?*
- *What have I learned so far?*

After Reading:

- *What was the author trying to teach me?*
- *What are some details?*
- *How did the photographs and captions help me understand more?*
- *Read the book again and look for the vocabulary words.*
- *What questions do I still have?*

Extension Activities:

- *What was your favorite part of the book? Write a paragraph on it.*
- *Draw a picture of your favorite thing you learned from the book.*

Table of Contents

WHAT IS BIG WAVE SURFING?

Big wave **surfing** is the art of surfing big waves. It is only practiced by very experienced surfers around the world.

Big wave surfing is a very dangerous type of surfing. Only surfers who love a pure **adrenaline** rush are brave enough to do this sport.

Big wave surfing began in the 1940s and 1950s. The first big wave surfers charged the huge waves at Makaha, Hawaii.

Fact

George Downing was one of the first surfers to surf big waves. He also designed the first big wave surfboard. Downing was inducted, or added, to the Surfers' Hall of Fame in 2011.

Fact

A surf break is a popular spot where people surf breaking waves. A wave breaks when its crest, or highest point, falls over onto itself.

Pioneers of big wave surfing pushed the limits by surfing some of the most feared surf breaks in Hawaii, California, and around the world.

WHO CAN BIG WAVE SURF?

Big wave surfing is not for everyone, but it is very exciting to watch. As with all types of surfing, a big wave surfer must be a great swimmer.

Big wave surfers are in excellent physical and mental shape. They need to be able to stay calm and hold their breath during a **wipeout**.

Fact

Yoga is a great way to increase strength, flexibility, and balance.

Big wave surfers do a great amount of preparation before taking on huge waves.

Fact

Many big wave surfers train by doing underwater rock running. This helps surfers strengthen their muscles and improves their ability to hold their breath underwater.

CHOOSING EQUIPMENT

As with every type of surfing, a **surfboard** and fins are the most important equipment.

Fact

A big wave surfboard is called a gun. These surfboards are longer, thicker, and can handle massive waves.

An inflatable life vest is a key piece of safety equipment. **Carbon dioxide** (CO2) canisters fill up air pockets in the vest to bring a surfer back to the water's surface quickly.

inflatable life vest $500–1,000

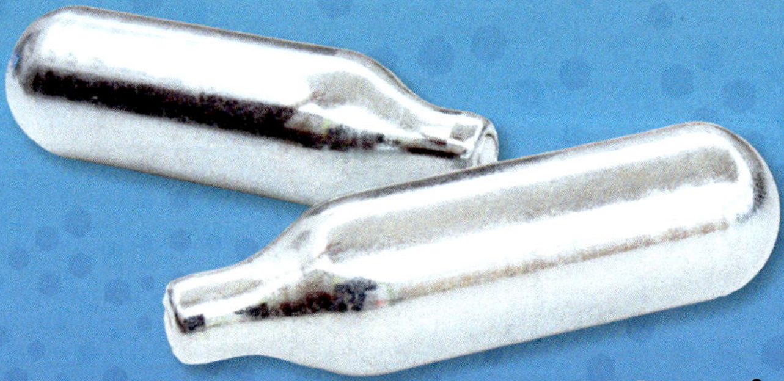

CO2 canisters $15–30

A big wave surfer may also decide to use a **wetsuit**, helmet, or **leash**. Surf wax and a traction pad can help keep the surfer from slipping off their board.

helmet $50–200

wetsuit $70–200

leash $30–50

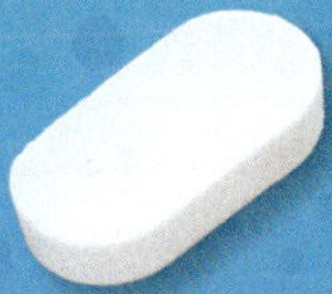

surf wax $5

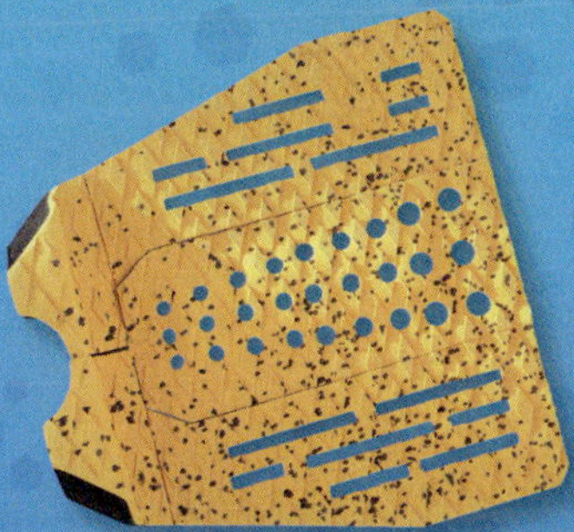

traction pad $30–80

WHERE TO BIG WAVE SURF

There are great places to big wave surf all around the world. Some of the biggest waves in the world are found in Hawaii.

Big waves are created by a combination of winds, **tides**, and the ocean floor. Earthquakes and hurricanes can produce big waves too, but surfers should only surf big waves when it is safe to do so.

Fact

The World Surf League (WSL) big wave competition season runs from November to March.

Fact

One of the deadliest surf breaks in the world is Pipeline, in Hawaii.

World-famous surf breaks include Jaws in Hawaii, Nazaré in Portugal, Mavericks in California, and Teahupo'o in Tahiti.

HOW TO BIG WAVE SURF

Big wave surfers must be highly experienced. Big wave surfing has a considerable risk of injury or even death.

With big waves comes big wipeouts. The power from a 20-foot (6-m) wave could push a surfer 50 feet (15 m) underwater, tossing them in every direction.

Big wave surfers must train themselves mentally for wipeouts. Keeping a calm mind is key for **survival**. It is important that a surfer does not panic when they are underwater.

Fact

Those who decide to try big wave surfing will need to take the time to train and prepare.

To get to a wave, a big wave surfer can paddle in or tow in.

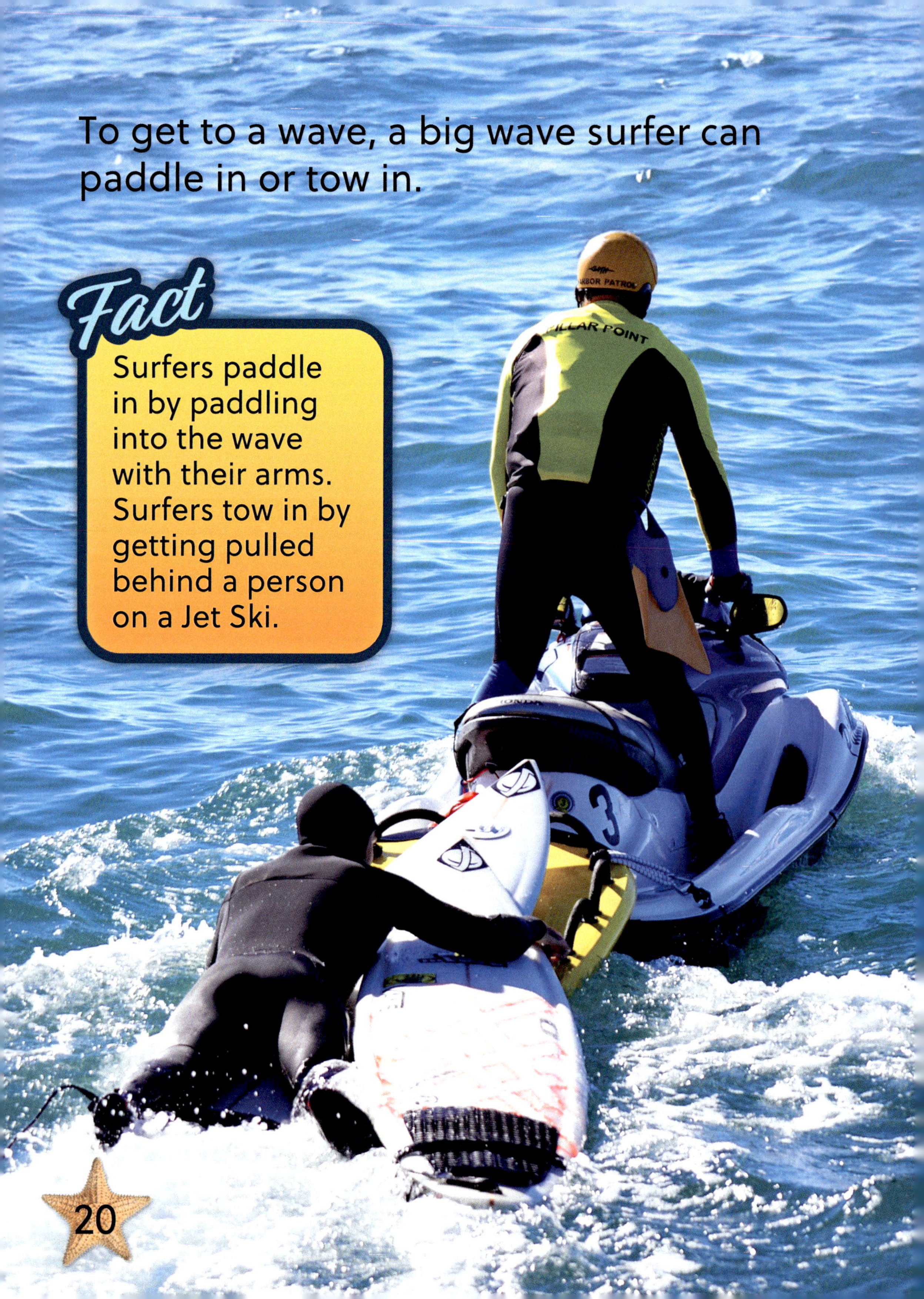

Fact

Surfers paddle in by paddling into the wave with their arms. Surfers tow in by getting pulled behind a person on a Jet Ski.

STAYING SAFE

Big wave surfers do many things to keep safe. However, there is still great risk with each wave they ride.

Fact

Physical and mental preparation are a must for keeping safe.

It is very important to wear an inflatable life vest. Wearing a helmet can help reduce the chances of a head injury.

Fact

40 percent of surf-related injuries involve the head.

Fact

Rescue boats with emergency medical technicians (EMTs) stand by at most big wave surf locations.

Big wave surfers do not surf alone. A Jet Ski driver plays an important role in big wave surfing. After a wipeout, a Jet Ski driver can rush in and pull the surfer out of harm's way and onto a lifeboard.

FAMOUS BIG WAVE SURFERS

Sebastian Steudtner, from Germany, holds the world record for surfing the biggest wave. He surfed a 93.73-foot (28.57-m) wave in Nazaré, Portugal.

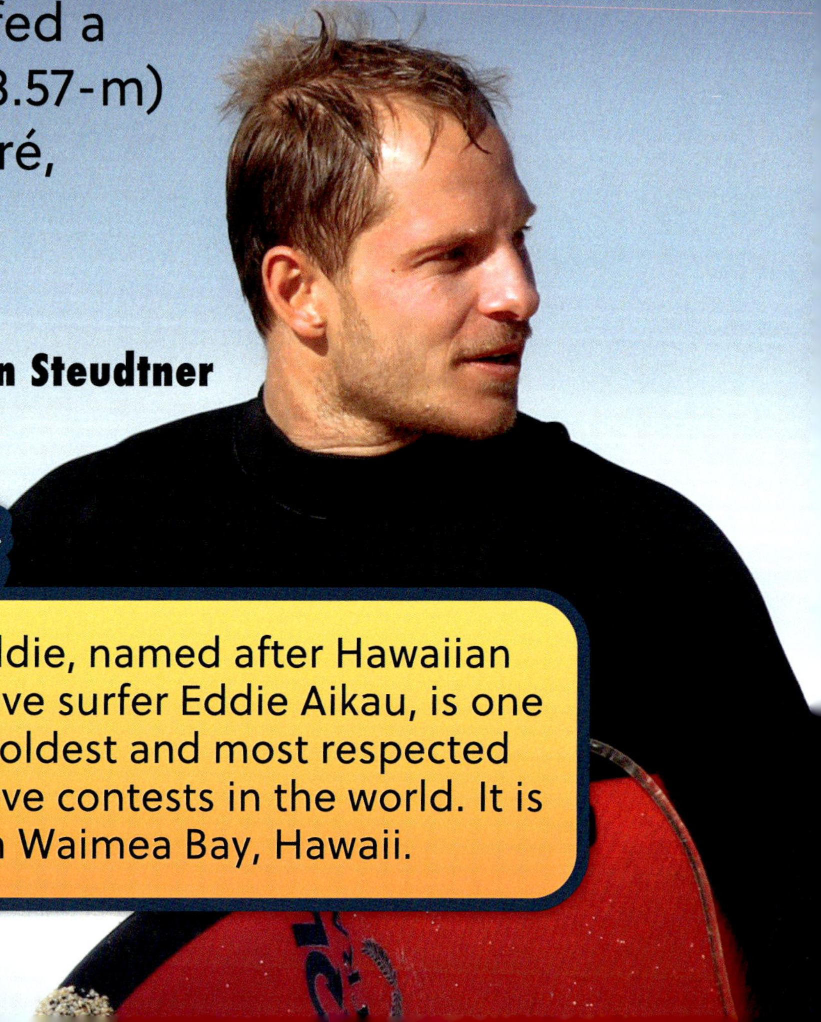

Sebastian Steudtner

Fact

The Eddie, named after Hawaiian big wave surfer Eddie Aikau, is one of the oldest and most respected big wave contests in the world. It is held in Waimea Bay, Hawaii.

Kai Lenny

Fact

In 2009, Carlos Burle claimed the first WSL Big Wave Tour title. Top big wave surfers today include Kai Lenny, Shane Dorian, and Maya Gabeira.

Carlos Burle

The World Surf League (WSL) considers big wave surfing a competitive sport. It hosts a men's and women's big wave tour each year.

RESPECTING OUR OCEANS

Respecting our oceans is very important. People all around the world depend on the ocean. For example, it generates more than half the oxygen we breathe.

Fact

More than 3 billion people rely on the ocean for food.

Picking up trash at the beach is a great way to show your respect for the ocean. This helps keep oceans clean.

Fact

Joining a local beach clean-up is a great way to help and meet other people who care about the ocean.

With more than 70 percent of our planet being covered by oceans, it is important that we do our part to protect them.

Big wave surfing is one of the most daring and challenging types of surfing. Although you may never get to try big wave surfing, it can be just as exciting to watch!

Glossary

adrenaline (uh-dren-uh-lin): A chemical that the body produces when it needs more energy or senses danger

carbon dioxide (KAHR-buhn dahy-OK-sahyd): A colorless and odorless gas found in air. Humans breathe in oxygen and breathe out carbon dioxide.

leash (leesh): A strap or cord that attaches a part of the body, such as an ankle, to the surfboard

pioneer (pye-uh-neer): One of the first people to investigate or work in a new area

surfboard (surf-bord): A long, narrow board with rounded ends on which surfers stand as they ride breaking waves

surfing (surf-ing): To balance on a surfboard and ride the crest of a breaking wave toward shore

survival (sur-vye-vuhl): To continue to live, especially after an accident or dangerous event

tides (tides): Constant changes in sea level caused by the pull of the Sun and the Moon on Earth

wetsuit (wet-soot): A close-fitting suit, usually made of a type of rubber called neoprene, that is worn in cold water to retain body heat

wipeout (wipe-out): A spill in some sport, such as a fall from a bicycle or being capsized on a surfboard

Index

Websites to Visit

https://education.nationalgeographic.org/resource/catching-biggest-wave/

https://www.redbull.com/us-en/history-of-big-wave-surfing

https://www.bigwavesurfing.com/how-big-wave-surfers-escape-underwater

https://www.surfer.com/how-to/surf-ultimate-beginners-guide-with-step-by-step-instructions

About the Author

Kerri Mazzarella was raised on the East Coast of southern Florida. Living near the beach has given her the opportunity to watch all types of surfing throughout her life. All four of her children have done their fair share of bodysurfing over the years for fun! Surfing is a great way to connect with the ocean and get some exercise. Her youngest son is a competitive shortboard surfer and travels all over the world to surf!

Written by: Kerri Mazzarella
Designed by: Bobbie Houser
Series Development: James Earley
Proofreader: Janine Deschenes
Educational Consultant: Marie Lemke M.Ed.

Photographs:
t = Top, c = Center, b = Bottom, l = Left, r = Right
Alamy: CI2: p. 6; Cavan Images: p. 10; ZUMA Press: p. 18-19; diebilderwelt: p. 24
Shutterstock: EpicStockMedia: cover, p. 1, 4, 15, 25; Sindo Novoa: p. 5; Christian Weber: p. 7; R.M. Nunes: p. 8; Sergey Furtaev: p. 9; Nikita M production: p. 11; Baloncici: p. 12 t; MisterStock: p. 12 b; Lilkin: p. 13 tl; dreii: p. 13 cl, bc; Photo Volcan: p. 13 bl; s-ts: p. 13 r; Christian Weber: p. 14; Phillip B. Espinasse: p. 16; Bruno Aleixo Photo: p. 17; Brian A. Witkin: p. 20; kudla: p. 21; Nao Novoa: p. 22; Silent O: p. 23; A.PAES: p. 25 cr; MATHILDE.LR: p. 26; GBJSTOCK: p. 27; Rich Carey: p. 28; Hiroshi-Mori-Stock: p. 29

Crabtree Publishing

crabtreebooks.com 800-387-7650

Printed in the U.S.A./052025/CP20250422

Published in Canada
Crabtree Publishing
616 Welland Ave.
St. Catharines, Ontario
L2M 5V6

Published in the United States
Crabtree Publishing
347 Fifth Ave
Suite 1402-145
New York, NY 10016

Library and Archives Canada Cataloguing in Publication
Available at Library and Archives Canada

Library of Congress Cataloging-in-Publication Data
Available at the Library of Congress

Hardcover: 978-1-0398-8029-0
Paperback: 978-1-0398-8389-5
Ebook (pdf): 978-1-0398-8149-5
Epub: 978-1-0398-8269-0